The Best websites FOR Home-work

ecommended Websites for Key Stage 3

Andy Seed

© 2006 Andy See...

Published in Great Britain in 2006 by Hodder Children's Books

Editor: Vic Parker

Design by Don Martin

Copyright ... Hodder Children's ...

The right of Andy See... to be identified as the Author of this Work
has been asserted by him in accordance with the Copyright, Designs
and Patents Act 1988.

A Catalogue record for this book is available from the British Library

ISBN-10: 0 340 93038 1
ISBN-13: 978 0 340 93038 0

Printed and bound in Great Britain by Bookmarque Ltd, Croydon, Surrey

The paper and board used in this paperback by Hodder Children's Books
are natural recyclable products made from wood grown in sustainable
forests. The manufacturing processes conform to the environmental
regulations of the country of origin.

Hodder Children's Books
a division of Hodder Headline Limited
338 Euston Road
London NW1 3BH

Contents

Introduction 4

English 7

Maths 23

Science 36

History 51

Geography 64

ICT 77

Design & Technology 85

Art 96

RE 107

Music 122

PE 131

Languages 140

PSHE & Citizenship 146

General Reference Sites 154

Top 10 Homework Tips 157

introduction

The web can be a great place to find out things but, let's face it, it's full of rubbish too. In fact, there's so much junk out there that you can waste hours – and that's no good at all if you've got homework to do. That's where this book comes in: it only contains good, helpful websites that have been carefully chosen by clever teacher-types to help you do your homework really well.

How do you use it? Just follow these tips to find the homework help you want and get the most out of the book:

- This book is divided into subjects and each subject is divided into the different topics you do at school. So first, check the Contents page at the front for the subject you want. Then turn to the subject pages and find the topic you need. For instance, if you want help with probability, first find *maths* in the Contents, then look in the *handling data* section for the pages on probability. But you can also find help with probability in many of the general maths sites listed, too. This is true for most other subjects as well.

- If the web address given for a site is very long, try to type it very carefully. It may be easier to search for the home page of the website then follow links to the page you want. For example, on page 7 the address for the *Fairground Spells* site is

www.channel4.com/learning/microsites/F/fairground/.

If you just type *channel 4* into your browser you'll get to the www.channel4.com home page. From there you can click *Learning*, then *Top Sites* then *Fairground Spells*.

- All of the websites are free but with just a few you may need to register or pay to see the full content. Ask at home if you think you need to do this for a particular site.

- Some of the websites listed have games and activities which require free software (called plugins), such as Flash, to play. Your computer probably has these already but if not, you can download them easily from many of the listed websites which have games.

- Some games and activities help you to understand a topic better, so even if you're just looking for facts and information, it may be worth having a go at a game or interactive quiz.

ENGLISH

Spelling and vocabulary

Funbrain

Pick easy or hard words, spot the duffer, then correct it. The hard ones are – well, hard.

www.funbrain.com/spell/

Fairground Spells

A set of very dinky little Flash spelling games to improve your wordpower. *Mole in the Hole* is a killer!

www.channel4.com/learning/microsites/F/fairground/

Skillswise: Spelling

Factsheets, worksheets, quizzes and games from the BBC. Top-quality material to help you improve a range of spelling skills and pick up good strategies.

www.bbc.co.uk/skillswise/words/spelling/

Homework High

This awesome site contains all sorts of really useful tips about spelling, written by teachers. Click on *English* then *Spelling Strategies* and browse through the questions.

www.channel4.com/learning/microsites/H/homeworkhigh/index.html

Spelling Rules

A complete list of spelling rules for nouns and verbs. Don't expect any graphics, wacky sounds or action: this is just solid, sound background info.

www2.gsu.edu/%7Ewwwesl/egw/susan.htm

Everyday Spelling

The navigation is slightly confusing but there are some helpful materials on this American site. Grade 6 is Year 7, Grade 7 is Year 8 and so on.

www.everydayspelling.com

Grammar & Punctuation

Guide to Grammar

Browse the drop-down menus to see just how comprehensive this site is.

http://grammar.ccc.commnet.edu/grammar

Introduction to Punctuation

A simple but well-written guide to punctuation marks and how to use them properly. Click on one of the 11 yellow icons to start.

www.edufind.com/english/punctuation/index.cfm

Commas Game

Stuck on when to use the dreaded comma? Here's a fun way to learn, with an interactive game and activity from the BBC.

www.bbc.co.uk/skillswise/words/grammar/punctuation/commas/game.shtml

Grammar Slammer

Basic help files on the things you need to know. Includes a glossary and a section on common mistakes in written English.

http://englishplus.com/grammar/index.htm

SOS Teacher

Click *English* then follow the links to the area you need help with. The site contains hundreds of teachers' answers to questions sent in by kids.

www.bbc.co.uk/schools/sosteacher/index.shtml

English Zone

There's plenty on this site, most of it in the form of short, 10-question interactive tests with feedback. It's a bit Americanised, but try the *Grammar Blast*.

http://english-zone.com/index.php

Grammar & Punctuation

BBC Bitesize: Sentences and Punctuation

The usual basic slide show presentation from the BBC followed by a short, challenging test. Give it a go.

www.bbc.co.uk/schools/ks3bitesize/english/writing/index.shtml

EnglishSpace

Some good animated learning activities about parts of speech – verbs, nouns, prepositions and adjectives. Try some of the other games too.

www.englishspace.ort.org/esdemo/startdemo_2.htm

Exploring English

A tidy guide to what's what in English. The design and navigation are nothing to shout about but try clicking *Style Elements* then *Punctuation* for help on apostrophes & co.

www.shared-visions.com/explore/english/english.html

Reading: fiction

Book Box

Top-notch stuff from Channel 4 learning: 30-plus quality children's authors and illustrators are featured with videos, extracts, games and interviews. Nice.

www.channel4.com/learning/microsites/B/bookbox/home.htm

Universal Teacher

You'll find useful online notes here about reading poetry and prose, and about reading for research information. Click *Key Stage 3* under *Tutorials* on the left of the page.

www.universalteacher.org.uk

Stories From the Web

All about books: reviews, games, competitions, information, tips, discussion and more.

www.storiesfromtheweb.org

Reading: Fiction

Bitesize: Reading

Basic input covering text types, finding information, character, atmosphere, language, sentences, paragraphs, structure and the writer's viewpoint. It has tests too.

www.bbc.co.uk/schools/ks3bitesize/english/reading/index.shtml

The Dickens Site

If you need to know about Chas, then this is the site. It has summaries of each of his novels with character profiles, notes, and tons more about the author too. Quality.

www.fidnet.com/%7Edap1955/dickens/

Jane Austen Info

This is comprehensive but the navigation is truly baffling. If you can decipher it you'll find biographical notes, novel synopses, annotated texts, and search facilities.

www.pemberley.com/janeinfo/janeinfo.html

Lord of the Flies: Education Pack

The Pilot Theatre Company has produced this useful set of notes about this book which you can download. It includes a summary, discussion of themes, character profiles and analysis of the story.

www.pilot-theatre.com/redesign/page.asp?idno=251

Lord of the Flies

Another primo site for this well-known William Golding novel, offering insights into various themes. There's a useful glossary of tricky words too.

www.gerenser.com/lotf/

Cool-Reads

Natty book-review site created and written by two teenagers. Reviews are split into short sections with star ratings and book-cover illustrations.

www.cool-reads.co.uk

Reading: Shakespeare

Bitesize: Shakespeare

Here you'll find summaries of *Henry V*, *Macbeth* and *Much Ado*, plus set scenes from the same three plays. Try the tests at the end to see if you're on the ball.

www.bbc.co.uk/schools/ks3bitesize/english

Talking To

Did you know that you can ask questions of Shakespeare, Dickens, Austen, Hardy, Orwell and other major authors, even though they're long dead and manky? You don't believe me? Look here.

www.talkingto.co.uk

Julius Caesar

Gives you a 'tour' of the play, breaking it down into acts and scenes, providing important questions notes. Hey – there are even pictures…

www.angliacampus.com/tour/sec/english/julius/index.htm

Reading: Poetry

E
N
G
L
I
S
H

Way With Words

Let Benjamin Zephaniah help you learn about poetry by looking at five very different poems. This brilliant microsite also covers fiction, non-fiction and drama.

www.channel4.com/learning/microsites/W/waywithwords/

Representative Poetry Online

Search poems by title, first line, poet's name or even key word. There is a timeline of poets, a criticism section and more. Coo.

http://rpo.library.utoronto.ca/

Beowulf in Cyberspace

There's no shortage of information and help here if you're studying this ancient poem. The site is a little random in terms of design but the resources it offers are top-drawer.

www.heorot.dk

📖 Reading: Poetry

ENGLISH

Poetry Zone

Poetry Zone mainly features contemporary poems and poets who specialise in funny rhymes. There are interviews, reviews, poems, tips for writing poetry and more.

www.poetryzone.ndirect.co.uk/index2.htm

Norman Nicholson: Five Poems

Click the arrow for *KS3 English* then *Norman Nicholson*. There's video footage plus audio of the poems being read aloud.

www.cleo.net.uk/subjects.php

Homework High: Poetry

Click *English* then *Poetry* to see over 1000 questions and answers about poetry. You can search for specific poems or authors too – well worth a go if you need help.

www.channel4.com/learning/microsites/H/homeworkhigh/

writing: General Advice

Skillswise: Writing Tips

Find out how to plan your writing, use paragraphs and proofread it: games, factsheets and worksheets.

www.bbc.co.uk/skillswise/words/writing/

Improving Your Writing

There's a lot of very helpful advice here on aspects of writing such as paragraphing and creating reports and recounts.

www.lancsngfl.ac.uk/curriculum/literacy/lit_site/html/writing/
writing_ict/cover.htm

Better Writing

Tips on using good grammar, writing effective letters, making your emails kick bottom, and more – from the publishers, Oxford.

www.askoxford.com/betterwriting/?view=uk

See also: Grammar and Punctuation, from page 10

ENGLISH

Writer's Toolkit

Sound advice on writing fiction including tips on openings, settings, characters, dialogue and endings.

www.storiesfromtheweb.org/sfwolderarea/write_it.asp

Writing With Writers

Goodly help from real authors about writing biographies, poems, folktales, mysteries, book reviews and even speeches.

http://teacher.scholastic.com/writewit/index.htm

Rhyming Dictionary

A brilliant tool if you're penning a poem and can't find that elusive rhyme for 'Llandudno' or 'haberdashery'.

www.rhymezone.com/

writing: for a specific purpose

Bitesize: Writing

Input on writing to inform/explain/describe, argue/persuade/advise, explore/imagine/entertain and analyse/review/comment. What more could you possibly want?

www.bbc.co.uk/schools/ks3bitesize/english/writing/index.shtml

Writing Instructions

Well-designed interactive page with advice and multiple choice activities to help you think about the nitty-gritty of writing instructions well.

www.englishonline.co.uk/englishnon/literacy/literacy11-14/instruct.html#1

Charities Index

Charities' websites are full of writing to persuade. Have a look at Oxfam, WWF, Christian Aid, RSPCA, War on Want to see how they do it.

www.paradigm-redshift.com/charity.htm

ENGLISH

Essay Writing

Let Factmonster advise you on the finer points of writing a winning essay. Everything is in short punchy points so you won't drop asleep reading it.

www.factmonster.com/homework/writingskills1.html

Paradigm Online

Some of this is a bit high-powered and challenging, but if you're after an A+, check out the advice on organising, revising and editing your writing.

www.powa.org

SATs Booster

Choose PDF or PowerPoint to get guidance about Y9 SATs in English. There is a set of tips about answering questions in the reading and writing tests.

www.y9booster.org.uk

maths

General Sites

Count On

Shedloads of decent games, activities, ideas, pictures, facts and even poems connected with numbers and maths. Don't miss it.

www.counton.org/

Maths Booster

A set of cool, noisy Flash games on all sorts of maths topics. The activities have help buttons and provide excellent practice.

www.bgfl.org/mathsbooster

Bitesize: Maths

Solid BBC help with numbers, algebra, data-handling, measures, shape and space, and mental arithmetic.

www.bbc.co.uk/schools/ks3bitesize/maths/

number and algebra

Nrich

If you like challenging puzzles which cover a really wide range of levels, you'll find this site enjoyable. There are hints and helpful explanations of solutions too.

www.nrich.maths.org

Skoool: Algebra

Click *KS3* then *Algebra* to see what this cool site has to offer. It has fab animated mini-lessons with audio and tests, with reviews.

http://lgfl.skoool.co.uk

Interactive Algebra

Tons of simple screens which show you how to solve different types of algebra problems. Just choose the area you want, try to do the question, then click *Answer* for the solution.

www.mathsnet.net/algebra/index.html

number and algebra

MATHS

Maths Zone

Funny microsite from Channel 4 where you have to help two smarmy brats escape from a dungeon by solving sneaky problems. Fun.

www.channel4.com/learning/microsites/M/mathszone/index.shtml

Skoool: Decimals

More excellent interactive teaching from Skoool, covering the multiplication, ordering and rounding of decimals. Click *KS3* then *Maths*, then scroll down to *21*.

http://lgfl.skoool.co.uk

Decimals

Cool Canadian site with slick animated activities on decimals. Click *Grade 6* then *Mathematics* then *Spy Guys*. When the page loads click *Lessons* then *Decimals*.

www.learnalberta.ca/Main.aspx

Multiplication.com

Still need to learn your tables? These online lessons aren't brilliant but they might just help you crack it.

www.multiplication.com/students.htm

MathsNet Fractions

Here is some nice interactive help with lovely fractions. You'll need to play around with the site first because it does look a bit complicated.

www.mathsnet.net/fractions/index.html

Visual Fractions

Help with adding, subtracting, multiplying, dividing fractions, or even just getting your head around them. The Java exercises it uses are effective.

www.visualfractions.com

number and algebra

Skill in Arithmetic

Basic and a bit cheesy (and American), but this site offers simple explanations of a wide range of number topics including decimals, ratio, percentages and powers of 10.

www.themathpage.com

Waldo's Equations

Wow – get Java working on your machine so you can play with Waldo's amazing equation activity: challenging and fun. Click *11-to-14* then *Equations*.

www.waldomaths.com

The Maths File Game Show

Some dinky Flash games from the BBC. They cover different aspects of number and algebra.

www.bbc.co.uk/education/mathsfile/index.shtml

Shape, Space and measures

Shapes

The graphics are good on this activity about the properties of 2-D and 3-D shapes. It includes nets of shapes to print out so you can make your own.

www.bgfl.org/bgfl/custom/resources_ftp/client_ftp/ks2/maths/3d/index.htm

Bitesize: Shape and Space

Notes and tests on shapes, symmetry, transformations and angles.

www.bbc.co.uk/schools/ks3bitesize/maths/shape_and_space/index.shtml

Skoool: Polygons

Don't miss these superior Flash presentations about symmetry, triangles and solids. Click KS3 then *Maths* then scroll down the page.

http://lgfl.skoool.co.uk

Shape, Space and Measures

MATHS

Virtual Tangram

Hours of fun sliding, flipping and making shapes with this simple activity. Includes a set of ideas to try.

www.amblesideprimary.com/ambleweb/mentalmaths/tangram.html

Convex Polyhedra with Regular Faces

Snappy title, huh? But if you need to know about the properties of 3-D shapes then this is the place to go. Click on the shapes to find out more.

www.liv.ac.uk/~spmr02/atm/poster.html

Skoool: Space

Awesome resources to enable you to get your nut round angles, rotation and transformation. Click *KS3* then *Maths* then scroll down the page.

http://lgfl.skoool.co.uk

Co-ordinates Games

Simple practice at using co-ordinates at different levels.

www.bgfl.org/bgfl/custom/resources_ftp/client_ftp/ks3/maths/coordinate_game/game1.htm

Enlargements

Waldo's superior Java applets can help you to understand better all sorts of maths including enlargements, angles and symmetry. Click *11-to-14* (you might also need to hit the *What To Do* button).

www.waldomaths.com

Pythagoras

More from the excellent Canadian Junior High Math. Click *Grade 7* then *Mathematics* then *Junior High Math* then *Pythagoras*. The videos are slow to download but worth it.

www.learnalberta.ca/Main.aspx

Shape, Space and measures

Surface Area and Volume

Click *Grade 7* then *Mathematics* then *Junior High Math* (it's Canadian) then *Surface Area and Volume* to find videos and clever interactives. Broadband essential.

www.learnalberta.ca/Main.aspx

Measures

Need assistance with perimeters, area or capacity? Never fear – Homework High is sure to have some answers for you. Click *Mensuration* or type your question.

www.channel4.com/learning/microsites/H/homeworkhigh/maths/index.jsp

Time Activities

This site has seven interactive activities on the theme of time, all connected with aircraft flights.

www.nwlg.org/pages/resources/mapgames/numeracy.html

Handling Data

Bitesize: Data Handling

Click *Handling Data* for slide presentations and tests on data collection and recording, representing data, averages, and probability. Good if you need a quick overview of one of these topics.

www.bbc.co.uk/schools/ks3bitesize/maths

Graphs

Mathsnet has kindly put together over 200 web-based activities to help you understand what graphs are all about. The least you could do is look at them, I reckon…

www.mathsnet.net/graphs/index.html

Straight Line Graphs

With this nifty piece of online kit you can shift a line and see the equation it plots change before your very eyes. Click *11-to-14* then *Straight Line Graphs*. Cunning.

www.waldomaths.com/

Handling Data

MATHS

Scatter Graphs

This is a free Flash sample lesson from a subscription site: it has good interactive features and will help you to understand the purpose of scatter diagrams.

www.mymaths.co.uk/samples/scatterGraphsLessonSample.swf

Skoool: Using Graphs

More expert online help from the Skoool site, this time on graphs. Click *KS3* then *Maths* then *Using Graphs*.

http://lgfl.skoool.co.uk

Data Display and Graphs

Quality video and interactives on graphing. Click *Grade 7* then *Mathematics* then *Junior High Math* then *7* then *Data Display and Graphs*. Broadband essential.

www.learnalberta.ca/Main.aspx

Interpreting Data

If you have trouble reading charts or finding averages then Homework High should be able to assist. Click *Interpreting Data* or type your question.

www.channel4.com/learning/microsites/H/homeworkhigh/maths/index.jsp

Brainteasers and Puzzles

Ok, so only some of these involve data handling, but they're nearly all good and will really get your grey cells fizzing.

http://puzzling.caret.cam.ac.uk

M-G6 Probability

Top site for learning about probability using animated presentations. Click *Grade 6* then *Mathematics* then *Spy Guys* then *Probability*.

www.learnalberta.ca/Main.aspx

science

Life Processes and Living Things

Skoool: Cells and Cell Functions

Go to Skoool if you want high-quality animated online lessons giving you the facts in a punchy, interactive way. Click *KS3* then *Biology* then *Cells* and *Cell Functions*.

http://lgfl.skoool.co.uk/index.aspx

School Science: Living Things

Good-quality input on loads of topics: life processes, health, the human body, reproduction, green plants, micro-organisms and many more.

www.schoolscience.co.uk/cgi-bin/col/searchlinks.pl

Planet Science

Facts, games, quizzes, information, news, resources and more. The navigation isn't great but it's quite funky and informative.

www.planet-science.com/home.html

Life Processes and Living Things

BBC Human Body

A variety of resources from the BBC including *Interactive Body*, which has games and demos covering topics such as organs, muscles, skeleton and puberty.

www.bbc.co.uk/science/humanbody

My Body

Top-notch noisy Flash site with a clickable body. Don't be put off because it looks a bit kiddyish – there are plenty of hard facts about organs, body systems and more.

www.kidshealth.org/kid/body/mybody.html

Digestion

A very detailed set of pages with lots of information; not much in the way of diagrams or photos, but a useful little test is included at the bottom of each page to see if you've been listening.

www.abpischools.org.uk/resources04/digestion/index.asp

The Heart and Circulation

This is a great site if you need detailed facts about the circulatory system. 10 pages, with simple interactive exercises included.

www.abpischools.org.uk/resources/heart/index.asp

Sciencepages

Well-organised materials divided into modules for each year from Y7-to-Y9. Includes useful activities on cells, reproduction, variation and classification, food and digestion, respiration, and microbes and disease.

www.sciencepages.co.uk/keystage3/keystage3.php

Food Chains

Drag the plants and animals into the correct position in the food chains – it's not easy. Do the *Feeding Relationships* activity first.

www.nwlg.org/pages/resources/blueplanet

Life Processes and Living Things

Homework High: Scientific Enquiry

This is the site where teachers answer children's homework questions. It has humungous amounts of helpful information on topics such as scientific enquiry.

www.channel4.com/learning/microsites/H/homeworkhigh/science/index.jsp

Bitesize: Photosynthesis

Stuck on photosynthesis? Hundreds of teachers' answers to questions about plants and other biology topics, complete with a handy search feature.

www.bbc.co.uk/schools/ks3bitesize/sosteacher/science/browse.shtml

ARKive

Monster searchable database of British wildlife plus endangered species around the world. Amazing quality movies, photos and information.

www.arkive.org

SciNet

Admirable, easy-to-suss site giving basic information about plants and the body among other topics. A good starting point for basic info.

www.nelsonthornes.com/secondary/science/scinet/scinet/index.htm

Biology4kids

Great stuff: a simple straightforward non-flashy site with tons of information and diagrams. It has sections on cells, micro-organisms, plants, vertebrates, invertebrates and animal systems.

www.biology4kids.com

Habitats

Learn about habitats, animal adaptation and survival with help from the World Wildlife Federation.

www.panda.org/news_facts/education/high_school/habitats/index.cfm

materials and Their properties

SCIENCE

Chem4kids

Get basic information on matter, elements, atoms, reactions and more. Not much in the way of graphics, but top notch for reference.

www.chem4kids.com

SciNet: Elements and Reactions

Simple, easy-to-follow, basic information about elements and reactions. There is a clickable periodic table and integrated glossary.

www.nelsonthornes.com/secondary/science/scinet/scinet/index.htm

Sciencepages

Straightforward science information with illustrations quizzes and links. Use the year group navigation (Y7-to-Y9) to find modules on acids and alkalis, plus atoms, compounds, elements and mixtures.

www.sciencepages.co.uk/keystage3/keystage3.php

Skoool: KS3 Chemistry

Try out this set of meaty learning resources from Skoool. Covers properties of materials, metals and non-metals, displacement reactions and more, with animated audio presentations plus tests and reviews.

http://lgfl.skoool.co.uk/keystage3.aspx?id=64

Interactive Periodic Table

Roll your mouse over each element for basic information.

www.schoolscience.co.uk/periodictable.html

The Challenge of Materials

Zappy pages from the Science Museum about making, using and selecting materials.

www.sciencemuseum.org.uk/on-line/challenge/index.asp

materials and their properties

Science Museum

A page of links to resources from the Science Museum which support homework and learning. Explore diverse topics such as energy, genes, space, the brain and nuclear power.

www.sciencemuseum.org.uk/education/student/school.asp

Bitesize: SOS Teacher

Browse or search through tons of questions and answers about materials. Try Homework High as well.

www.bbc.co.uk/schools/ks3bitesize/sosteacher/science/browse.shtml

www.channel4.com/learning/microsites/H/homeworkhigh

Doc Brown's Chemistry Clinic

Try Doc Brown's ingenious interactive KS3 quizzes. Lots of good diagrams included and you get feedback for each answer. Read the notes first!

www.wpb4.btinternet.co.uk/page12/page12.htm

Bitesize: Chemistry

This is good if you need a basic summary or introduction to a topic. Make sure you do the test at the end and keep doing it until you get full marks!

www.bbc.co.uk/schools/ks3bitesize/science/chemistry

The Rock Cycle

Goodly page of facts about rocks, covering topics such as weathering and erosion, types of rocks and rock formation.

www.moorlandschool.co.uk/earth/rockcycle.htm

People and Discoveries

A simple site with a page for each of the last century's greatest scientists, from Luis Alvarez to the Wright brothers.

www.pbs.org/wgbh/aso/databank/bioindex.html

Physical Properties

Circuit World

Build and test your own circuits using drag-and-drop symbols. Click the arrow for *KS3* and *Science* to start. Save and print your circuit or reveal the components. Fab.

www.cleo.net.uk/subjects.php

Tech Topics: Electricity

This site has a high-quality animated guide to electricity, although it's a bit too clever at times. Definitely worth a look though.

www.thetech.org/exhibits/online/topics/topics.html

Electricity and Magnetism

Noisy Flash-based site which uses animated slides to take you through the stuff you need to know. Slightly cheesy graphics and effects, but they mean well.

http://ippex.pppl.gov/interactive/electricity

Power Up!

A site which is primarily concerned with electrical safety but includes a lot of helpful information about circuits, current and electricity generation too.

www.electricityineducation.co.uk/keystage3/index.html

Forces

Well-presented introduction to forces and other KS3 physics topics such as light, sound and magnetism. Better for Y7 than Y9 though.

www.zephyrus.co.uk/welcometophysics.html

Forces Lab

Cool little piece of webbery which allows you to see forces at work. Decide whether to compress, bend, stretch, slide or twist, then move the slider to see what happens.

www.pbs.org/wgbh/buildingbig/lab/forces.html

Physical Properties

SciNet: Light

Tidy chunks of information here with some good graphics. The navigation is wonderfully simple and the glossary's a bonus. Also has info on electricity.

www.nelsonthornes.com/secondary/science/scinet/scinet/index.htm

Bitesize: Physics

Covers electricity, magnetism, forces, light, sound, the Earth and beyond, energy resources and transfer. Don't expect much in the way of depth.

www.bbc.co.uk/schools/ks3bitesize/science/physics

School Science Links

Well-organised links to physics topics including electricity, magnetism, forces and motion, light and sound, the Earth and beyond, and energy. Just make sure you use the KS3 links and not KS4.

www.schoolscience.co.uk/cgi-bin/col/searchlinks.pl

Think-Energy

British Gas have kindly laid on this interactive site and it's not at all bad – it certainly covers a wide area of energy topics. Click *11-to-14* to start then *Online Activities*.

www.think-energy.com

Energy Resources

A superb set of illustrated notes from science teacher, Andy Darvill, all about energy resources – from fossil fuel to biomass. Includes worksheet and quiz.

www.darvill.clara.net/altenerg/index.htm

SOS

Secondary Online Science from Channel 4 Learning has a number of Flash games on the theme of energy. A good way to learn about fuels, energy resources and energy efficiency.

www.channel4.com/learning/microsites/S/sos/

Physical Properties

Our Solar System

The design is grim but if you can ignore this and the irritating ads, there is stacks of helpful information here.

www.enchantedlearning.com/subjects/astronomy

Virtual Tour of the Solar System

Excellent Shockwave trip around our sun, the planets, comets, moons and more, with all sorts of ace features such as planet cams and zoom buttons.

www.scienceyear.com/planet10/solar_preload.html

How Stuff Works

Interesting site which covers all sorts of bizarre topics under the banner of science. Make sure you don't get tricked into clicking the sneaky shopping or ad links.

http://science.howstuffworks.com/

History

Britain: 1066–1500

Medieval England

Reliable source of information and images covering monarchs, battles, castles, the feudal system, the Domesday book, the Black Death and much more.

www.historylearningsite.co.uk/england_medieval.htm

Medieval Life

Plenty of background facts here, including much on everyday aspects of life (food, farming, houses), plus quizzes and links.

www.historyonthenet.com/Medieval_Life/medievallifemain.htm

The Time Traveller's Guide to Medieval Britain

Something a bit different from Channel 4, covering themes like words, hazards, sex and sleaze (!), class, and movers and shakers. The info is good but there's a sorry lack of graphics.

www.channel4.com/history/microsites/H/history/guide12/index.html

Medieval Realms

Well thought-out resource from the British Library with mini-projects on Thomas Becket and women's lives. Gives you access to a top collection of pictures, documents, maps and other sources.

www.bl.uk/services/learning/curriculum/medrealms.html

Norman Conquest

The pages are a bit cluttered, but this useful site does take you through the key elements of the Norman conquest in some style, with various interactive elements along the way.

www.normanconquest.co.uk

Essential Norman Conquest

There are some clever features on this site such as animated maps and an interactive timeline. Give it a go – it's certainly not boring history…

www.essentialnormanconquest.com

Britain: 1500 – 1750

Tudor History

Simple navigation, lots of information, images, maps, glossary, references, chronology, and lots of links to more sources. What more could you want?

www.tudorhistory.org

Life in Elizabethan England

Wow! If you're after specific information about everyday life in this period then you should find it here.

www.renaissance.dm.net/compendium/home.html

The Making of the United Kingdom

This site consists of links to other sites on specific aspects of Britain 1500–1750. The websites linked to it are very variable, but there are plenty of good ones. There are also quizzes, a student forum, games and a search facility.

www.schoolhistory.co.uk/year8links

The English Civil War

Weapons, Cromwell, battles, weapons, key figures, Royalists, Parliamentarians – it's all here, even if the graphics are a bit iffy.

www.historyonthenet.com/Civil_War/civilwarmain.htm

Kings and Queens Since 1603

The monarchy's own website brings you a potted history of kings and queens, with portraits and a few interesting documents to look at.

www.royal.gov.uk/output/Page13.asp

The Plague

Facts, pics, docs and links all about the 1665 outbreak, concentrating on London and the spread of this big-momma lurgy to the rest of the country.

www.channel4.com/history/microsites/H/history/plague/index.html

Britain: 1750 – 1900

HISTORY

The Industrial Revolution

Links to several non-flashy pages covering factories, mines, industrial town life, Arkwright, Watt, children, and factory laws.

www.historylearningsite.co.uk/indrevo.htm

Industrialisation

Find out how Britain was transformed in the eighteenth and nineteenth centuries with the machine age. The site includes Flash games and other activities.

www.bbc.co.uk/history/society_culture/industrialisation

Freedom: the Transatlantic Slave Trade

Good e-learning resource from the national Maritime Museum, with access to original documents, plus plenty of facts and useful images.

www.nmm.ac.uk/freedom

History Trail – the Victorians

Tidy micro-site from the BBC with articles, games and quizzes on the themes of industrialisation, social conditions and Victorian women.

www.bbc.co.uk/history/lj/victorian_britainlj/index.shtml

Victorians

What was it like to live in a Victorian city or work in a factory? If you don't know, have a look here. Quite a choccy-centric website, it has to be said.

www.cadburylearningzone.co.uk/history/index.htm

Virtual Tour of HMS Victory

Have an online shufti round Nelson's fantastic flagship. The quality photos are accompanied by detailed facts.

www.stvincent.ac.uk/Heritage/1797/Victory/index.html

A European Study before 1914

HISTORY

The Roman Empire

The navigation is a little confusing here but you'll find a solid core of information and a few carefully chosen pictures. Not a lot in the way of interaction, though.

www.pbs.org/empires/romans/index.html

Romans Links

A page of links sites where you can research the Romans.

www.schoolhistory.co.uk/year7links/romans.shtml

Renaissance Connection

A nice Monty Python-style opening animation introduces you to this tasty little site, which focuses on art and artists.

www.renaissanceconnection.org/

The Renaissance

Basic website with a focus on the Italian city of Florence and a set of web links. Helpful if you want a brief overview of this period.

www.learner.org/exhibits/renaissance

Homework High

Click *European Study before 1914* to see 518 questions with teachers' answers about topics such as Napoleon, the crusades, the Renaissance, explorers and the French Revolution.

www.channel4.com/learning/microsites/H/homeworkhigh/history/index.jsp

Napoleon's Empire

Interesting site from Channel 4, high on text but low on graphics. Covers themes such as the arts, sciences, customs, revolution, words and people 1799–1815.

www.channel4.com/history/microsites/H/history/guide18/index.html

A World Study Before 1900

Native Americans

Links to sites where you can learn about the history of Native Americans.

www.schoolhistory.co.uk/year8links/native.shtml

First Americans

Comprehensive, interesting and occasionally baffling site about the history, culture and traditions of Native Americans, complete with activities and audio facility.

www.ic.arizona.edu/ic/kmartin/School

Black Peoples of America

Basic site covering topics including slavery, plantations, segregation and civil rights. There are also quizzes and even a wordsearch if you're bored.

www.historyonthenet.com/Slave_Trade/slaverymain.htm

Islamic Civilisations

Short sections on Arab expansion, Baghdad, and the crusades, among others – the content is a bit thin, though.

www.schoolshistory.org.uk/Islamic%20Civilisations.htm

Islamic Civilisations Links

This site recommends websites for various KS3 topics and has several other features including a students' forum, games, quizzes and online lessons.

www.schoolhistory.co.uk/year7links/islamic.shtml

The Incas

Long, text-heavy page about the Incas. Search for the few links on the page to find out more.

www.millville.org/Workshops_f/Acker_Inca/inca.htm

A World Study After 1900

The Great War

Superlative site devoted to the First World War. Gazillions of original sources, case studies with key questions, background info, great photos and documents plus worksheets.

www.learningcurve.gov.uk/greatwar/default.htm

World War I

The site says, 'Read and listen to stories of the War from the people who lived it. Explore diaries, letters, scrapbooks, newspaper cuttings, photos and keepsakes.' Recommended.

www.bbc.co.uk/schools/worldwarone

The First World War

Learn about the War's causes, its events, principle figures and conclusion. With glossary, biographies and links.

www.channel4.com/history/microsites/F/firstworldwar

Women at War

Steady but unspectacular site with photos, text, stories and movies. Gives a good overview of the new roles that women took on during the war.

http://caber.open.ac.uk/schools/stanway/index.html

The Home Front

Learn about the impact of World War II in Britain with this excellent, media-rich site. Activities, videos, information, pictures and access to original sources.

www.learningcurve.gov.uk/homefront/default.htm

Scientific Inventions

Learn about significant inventions since 1900 including plastic, computers, the jet engine, TV, atomic power, antibiotics and aircraft. Nice and uncluttered.

www.historylearningsite.co.uk/scientific_inventions_1900.htm

Geography

General Sites

Internet Geography

A brilliant place if you need a quick introduction to a particular topic. There are basic notes, diagrams and animations and photos too – a tasty free resource.

www.geography.learnontheinternet.co.uk

The Geography Site

Another stonking-good free site covering a wide range of topics. It has detailed notes, excellent photos and even a page of geographical jokes (warning: they're terrible).

www.geography-site.co.uk

GeoResources

A good place to look if you can't find specific information elsewhere. It has resources on 20 KS3 geography topics plus links to sites on countries.

www.georesources.co.uk/indexks3.htm

General Sites

Homework High

Click *Geography* to see hundreds of answers to homework questions about geography topics from tectonic processes to population.

www.channel4.com/learning/microsites/H/homeworkhigh

The World Factbook

Let the CIA give you the lowdown on just about every country on Earth. Includes such essential stats as population, land use, birth rate and rather more off-road data such as international disputes and airfields with unpaved runways.

www.odci.gov/cia/publications/factbook/index.html

World Atlas

The navigation is a pain but this American site does have lots of maps, including outline maps you can print, as well as information about countries. Beware lurking ads though.

www.worldatlas.com

Physical Processes

Earth Science

Admirable school site covering earth structure, plate tectonics, the rock cycle, volcanoes and earthquakes, and our atmosphere, amongst other topics. Try it.

www.moorlandschool.co.uk/earth/index.htm

Geo Mysteries

Don't be put off by naff cartoon pal 'Rex the Dino Detective', this site is a smart way to learn about rock formation. It's graphic-rich with Flash animations and a useful geological timeline.

www.childrensmuseum.org/geomysteries/index2.html

Earth Structure

Simply presented and illustrated basic facts about rocks, tectonics, volcanoes, earthquakes and more. The site also covers other physical geography topics.

www.geography4kids.com

Physical Processes

Volcano World

Claims to be the world's premier volcano site but the navigation is definitely dodgy and it has broken links. However, you will find plenty of information and some spectacular photos if you search hard.

www.volcanoworld.org

Ideers

The aim of this site is 'To communicate the challenge and excitement of earthquake engineering research to young people'. It has lots of good information on earthquakes.

www.ideers.bris.ac.uk/meta/aboutus.html

Virtual Fieldwork

Four fantastic units about coastal erosion, sand dunes, a river study and an urban study. Includes maps, background information, photos, notes and more.

www.georesources.co.uk/indexvf.htm

Rivers and Coasts

Useful and fairly comprehensive introduction to these two topics from the BBC. It's slightly annoying because you have to do so much clicking to work through the slides but the animations are good.

www.bbc.co.uk/schools/riversandcoasts/index.shtml

Coastal Landforms

Impressive media-rich site in the form of a set of slides. There are numerous maps, diagrams, explanations and some videos to explain the processes which have shaped the coast.

www.angliacampus.com/tour/sec/geog/coastal/index.htm

A Virtual Geography Journey

This site has a handy animated presentation of the hydrological cycle, plus pages on settlements, pollution, rivers, floods and coasts.

www.nwlg.org/pages/resources/geog/hydro_cycle/index.htm

Weather and Climate

Met Office

The place to go for detailed weather information. Includes good explanations of atmospheric phenomena, plus case studies of events, and details of forecasting and weather observing.

www.meto.gov.uk/education/secondary/students/index.html

Weather

Click Y8 to see a collection of Word documents and PowerPoint presentations about weather. Some are aimed at teachers but you will find a lot which are useful.

www.learngeography.net

Climate Change

Click *Climate Change* under the *What We Do* menu to discover background facts on climate change plus details of possible solutions proposed by the World Wildlife Fund.

www.panda.org/index.cfm

Ecosystems

Deserts

This is Oxfam's basic and helpful guide to desert environments. You need to click *Site A-Z* then scroll down to find deserts. It also has a similar section on rainforests and lots of info about disasters.

www.oxfam.org.uk/coolplanet

Dartmoor

Click *Factsheets and Leaflets* to access or download stacks of facts about this important UK upland environment.

www.dartmoor-npa.gov.uk/learningabout.html

Cloud Forest Alive

Natty site about the beautiful cloud forests of Central America. Listen to the eerie howler monkeys, see a hummingbird-cam and also get hard facts about this special environment.

www.cloudforestalive.org

GEOGRAPHY

Popinfo

Covers population issues and helps you to think about how they are connected with sustainability, poverty, consumption, conflict and other big themes. A little heavy-going but well presented.

www.popinfo.org

Virtual Tour of Birmingham

Well constructed scoot around Brum with interactive map, photos, glossary and information. Click *Humanities and Community*, then *Geography*, then scroll down to *KS3* to see the link to the tour.

www.bgfl.org

World Infozone

Truckloads of information about countries here – and much more than just bare stats. Covers (in limited detail) themes such as architecture, food, health, technology, religion and sport.

www.worldinfozone.com

Development

Global Eye

Excellent site which focuses on development issues. Each issue is devoted to one particular developing country (and includes data comparing it to the UK) along with one key topic such as water or aid.

www.globaleye.org.uk

Kenya

A simple set of illustrated pages from a school site about this African country, covering human and physical aspects.

www.hewett.norfolk.sch.uk/CURRIC/NEWGEOG/Kenya/kenya.htm

Sustainable Development

A quality interactive site featuring farming, tourism, transport, settlements and manufacturing in Northern Ireland. Some dinky Flash animations included.

www.bbc.co.uk/northernireland/schools/11_16/ks3geography/index.shtml

GEOGRAPHY

Renewable Energy

Top-quality government site about the eight renewable energy sources currently being used and researched in the UK. Info, pics, links and downloads are available.

www.dti.gov.uk/renewables/schools

Planet.com

Covers global issues, environmental themes, and sustainable development, with strands on water, money, food and farming, energy, biodiversity, cars, and natural resources. Includes videos, games, puzzles and action points.

www.channel4.com/learning/microsites/P/planet/menu.html

Global Warming

Click *12-to-16* first then use the simple navigation to extract facts, try activities or a quiz, and investigate the links.

www.defra.gov.uk/environment/climatechange/schools/index.htm

Encyclopedia of the Atmospheric Environment

Snappy title, eh? But if you need to know about climate change, acid rain, ozone depletion, global warming and air-quality issues, this is the place. It's just a bit lacking in graphics.

www.ace.mmu.ac.uk/eae

Your Ocean

Really interesting site from the National Maritime Museum challenging people to think about the ocean and how it is affected by energy, waste and climate change.

www.nmm.ac.uk/upload/package/52/index.html

Water in Schools

This site covers all sorts of ground but the *World Water* pages (click *Microsites* first) are definitely worth looking at if you want a global picture.

www.waterinschools.com

map and Geography Skills

Mapzone

Fun, informative and well-designed, this site from Ordnance Survey is a must if you need help with map skills. There are facts, activities, games, animations and, er, maps.

www.mapzone.co.uk

Map Machine

Lets you select different types of maps which can be customised and printed. Includes conservation, topography, political, population density, and satellite views among other categories.

http://plasma.nationalgeographic.com/mapmachine

Multimap

Awesome site for maps at different scales: just type in a place or postcode then click to zoom. The aerial photo feature is extremely cool and the site now covers Europe and the world as well as the UK.

http://uk.multimap.com

iCT

General Sites

ICT

Do I.T.

A very useful, free online course introducing ICT and its different aspects: hardware, software, computer languages, information systems, networks and the internet.

http://doit.ort.org

Computer Lessons for Kids

This looks a bit crummy but it's actually a well-written and helpful introduction to what computers are and how they work.

www2.magmacom.com/~dsleeth/kids/lessons/starter.htm

Web Monkey

Build a website and use Web Monkey's tools to make slide shows, invitations or work with graphics.

http://webmonkey.wired.com/webmonkey/kids/

Computing.net

This is a site full of forums about fixing computer problems, but it does have some useful features worth exploring, such as a set of simple 'how to' guides.

http://computing.net/howto

ICT Teacher

This site has an ICT glossary and includes a set of brief tutorials showing you some nifty tricks with various types of software.

www.ictteacher.com

Dance Mat Typing

Want to touch-type? Then try this funky BBC mini-course with 12 lessons and a great comedy Scouse commentary.

www.bbc.co.uk/schools/typing/

Software Skills

Mission Control Centre

A set of online tasks, with a dodgy-but-fun spy theme. You can use these to brush up on general computer skills plus use of word-processing, spreadsheets, databases and presentation software.

www.teachict.co.uk/ks3_spy_project/missioncontrol.htm

IT Tips

School site which contains a helpful IT glossary, plus tips for using Word and Excel.

www.hewett.norfolk.sch.uk/curric/it/tips/tipmenu.htm

PowerPoint in the Classroom

This is a slick and attractive step-by-step guide to getting a PowerPoint presentation on the road and adding all those annoying features like crashing sounds and flying moose animations.

www.actden.com/pp

The internet

The Internet

A brief guide to the internet including information about how it works. The site includes videos and other pages about computers.

www97.intel.com/discover/JourneyInside/TJI_Internet/default.aspx

The Internet Explained

This is like a limited glossary but with detailed entries, explaining terms such as 'filter' and 'encryption'.

www.nch.org.uk/information/index.php?i=211

A Beginner's Web Glossary

If you don't know a GIF from a GUI, or what a firewall does, then you will probably find this guide helpful.

www.webteacher.org/windows.html

The internet

ICT

Searching the Web

Tips on searching the worldwide web from BBC Webwise. It's in the form of questions and answers, but you'll manage.

www.bbc.co.uk/webwise/askbruce/articles/search/index.shtml

Finding Information on the Internet

Excellent advice, including a section called *Googling to the Max*, which tells you how to get the most out of Google and other search engines.

www.lib.berkeley.edu/TeachingLib/Guides/Internet/FindInfo.html

Quick

This is a very good idea: a site designed to help you evaluate websites you come across when researching on the internet. 'Quick' stands for 'Quality Information Checklist'.

www.quick.org.uk/index2.htm

GetNetWise

Facts about internet safety, spam, viruses, hackers, spyware and protecting personal information.

www.getnetwise.org

Web Design Resources

A simple page with lots of links to useful sites and help documents which can be downloaded.

www.thekjs.essex.sch.uk/yates/web_design_links.htm

Think U Know

Funkily designed site all about safety in chatrooms and the dangers of the internet.

www.thinkuknow.co.uk

USEFUL GRAPHICS

ICT

Freefoto

Nearly 80,000 images organised into categories which you can use for various school ICT projects and to enhance homework.

www.freefoto.com/index.jsp

DK ClipArt

Top-quality illustrations and photos from Dorling Kindersley.

http://uk.dk.com/static/cs/uk/11/clipart/home.html

Discovery ClipArt

Nice little piccies arranged into categories such as food, technology, science, art and so on.

http://school.discovery.com/clipart/index.html

Design
& Technology

General Sites

Design-Technology

The layout and navigation of this site are a bit haphazard, to put it mildly, but it has an awesome collection of links organised by DT themes.

www.design-technology.info

DesignandTech.com

A rich source of information. The site has some pages of its own about materials and processes, and also hundreds of really well-chosen links to helpful pages on other sites relating to DT elements.

www.designandtech.com/

Technology Student

This amazingly detailed and comprehensive site is very much aimed at GSCE tech students but is also a great reference resource for KS3. Well worth browsing – the navigation is simple too.

www.technologystudent.com

D&T Online

The intro says, 'D&T Online is a site offering free access to a wide range of design and technology materials, resources and software for pupils to use as they engage in design and technology activities as part of the UK National Curriculum.' The illustrated information sections are invaluable.

www.dtonline.org

Design Technology Department

The layout and navigation of this site are a bit random but it does have some useful sections, especially the ones on packaging, hardwoods and bridges. There are also revision sheets.

www.design-technology.org

Technology Links

If you can't find what you're looking for D&T-wise elsewhere, then try this site of links, helpfully organised into themes.

http://technologylinks.org/

materials

Materials By Design

If you want to know about the five major classes of materials, or what a spacecraft is made from, then this is a good place to go. Don't be put off by the dull presentation.

www.mse.cornell.edu/courses/engri111//toc.htm

Hands On Plastics

Information about the history, structure, uses and characteristics of polymers, tidily presented.

www.handsonplastics.com/hands_on_plastics/index.html

Wood Characteristics

Everything you ever wanted to know about oak, balsa and mahogany but were afraid to ask.

www.woodbin.com/ref/wood/

Textiles Online

Snappy Flash-based site with some good games and an annoying search system for finding information. Focuses on environmental topics such as textile design, recycling and sustainability.

www.e4s.org.uk/textilesonline

Things We Wear

Another good interactive Flash site from the BBC to help you learn about clothing: fabrics, colours, materials and processes.

www.bbc.co.uk/scotland/education/as/tech/flash/index.shtml

The Packaging Education Programme

Lots of useful facts about packaging, complete with timeline, glossary and case studies. This otherwise commendable site is let down though by a mystifying lack of illustrations, especially on the case study pages.

www.incpen.org/education/edframe.htm

Design

RealDesign

Cool site from Channel 4, presenting case studies to show how designers go about their work creating new products. Flash animations, videos, design A-Z, useful info and a design toolkit interactive.

www.channel4.com/learning/microsites/R/realdesign/index_flash.html

British Standards Institution

The BSI is mainly concerned with ensuring health and safety through good design – have a go at their challenging playground activity game to get an insight into this. Click *11-to-14* first.

www.bsieducation.org/Education/default.php

Bad Designs

I love this site. It's a brilliant collection of real objects with naff design features. The photos and text are an excellent way of learning about mistakes to avoid when planning something.

www.baddesigns.com/index.shtml

structures and mechanisms

Build a Bridge

Find out why the Tacoma Narrows suspension bridge was destroyed by a 42mph wind and learn much more on this well-written introduction to bridges.

www.pbs.org/wgbh/nova/bridge/build.html

Mechanical Monkey

There are some superlative mechanical wooden toys on this commercial site – it should give you some good ideas for using cams, levers, belts, pulleys etc.

www.mechanicalmonkey.co.uk

How Stuff Works

What's in a TV? How does a laser printer print? Why are vacuum cleaners so noisy? Lots of answers on this ace site, but watch out for the sneaky ads and shopping links.

www.howstuffworks.com/

DESIGN & TECHNOLOGY

For much more on structures and mechanisms see General Sites, page 86

Working with food

Taste of Success

Here's a good resource for finding out about the development and production of food products in the real world. See how a Sainsbury's Italian ready-meal is put together.

www.j-sainsbury.co.uk/tasteofsuccess

British Nutrition Foundation

Click *Education* then *Cook Club* then *Secondary School Recipes* to see some — well, recipes. The site also has information about nutrition, food equipment and skills.

www.nutrition.org.uk

Flour and Grain

All the facts you'll ever need about flour and grain, plus some good recipes and reference material about food in general.

http://www.flourandgrain.com/homework/index.html

Foodlink

This is all about food safety – it's very good too, with an extensive glossary, food fact files, hygiene tips, info on safe preparation and storage, plus games including a quiz and *Calamity Kitchen*.

www.foodlink.org.uk

Safe Food

Another comprehensive food safety site, this time from Australia. Its *Bug Bible* gives you the lowdown on all the nasties lurking in your grub.

www.safefood.net.au

Warburtons

If you're lucky enough to be working on the Year 9 QCA Design and Technology units 'designing for markets' or 'quality production' then hopefully you'll find these pages rather handy.

www.warburtons.co.uk/curriculum/

miscellaneous

Warren Quizzes

Try these challenging KS3 design and technology quizzes from the Warren School. There is also a gallery of work and some other useful resources.

www.the-warren.org

Technology Insight

The idea of this site is to provide DT students with virtual visits to industry to see how products are developed, tested and manufactured. The design's a bit dodgy but there's some excellent content.

www.technology.org.uk/

Electronics: An Online Guide for Beginners

A good basic guide with plenty of detail, and quite well set out. There is a set of projects to try at the end.

http://library.thinkquest.org/16497/

Doctronics

Outstanding introduction and resources for electronics. Explanations, diagrams, information, projects, design files, photos and more.

www.doctronics.co.uk/design.htm

Robot Constructor

Build an online robot with this tasty Flash game, then overcome various hazards to collect cubes. The idea is that you'll learn plenty about robotics while having tons of fun.

www.channel4.com/science/microsites/R/robots/constructor.html

Robotics

This informative and well-illustrated site uses an interactive slide-show form of presentations with a 'next' button. It has animations, photos and lots to think about too.

http://www.thetech.org/exhibits/online/robotics/

Art

investigating Art

Blast Art

Chic BBC site aimed at 13-to-19s, covering
many aspects of art and featuring articles, galleries,
chatroom, messageboard, links, and an excellent
set of profiles of all kinds of artists.

www.bbc.co.uk/blast/art

Artisancam

Learn about the work of various living artists
through videos of artists at work, showing how
they carry out different techniques, plus much
more. Not to be missed.

www.artisancam.com

Study Art

A brilliant illustrated glossary of elements of art,
principles, artists, styles and media, plus a glossary.
Well worth a shufti.

www.sanford-artedventures.com/study/study.html

investigating Art

A R T

A. Pintura, Art Detective

Great idea: solve the mystery of Grandpa's painting by following the clues and answering questions. A satisfying way to learn about pictures.

www.eduweb.com/pintura/index.html

Inside Art

The idea of being sucked inside a Van Gogh painting might sound a bit cheesy, but this is a fun way to learn about styles, techniques and other elements of painting.

www.eduweb.com/insideart/index.html

Impressionism

Imaginatively presented introduction to this important art movement. Click *Experience Impressionism* then move through the slides.

www.impressionism.org

Art from India

Simple, well-illustrated and interesting school site. The resource covers a number of themes and is available at two reading levels.

www.hitchams.suffolk.sch.uk/india_art/index.htm

Artedventures

How do the Americans do it? The name is awful, and the cartoon chameleon guide is so cheesy, but the content of these interactive activities is great. A fun way to learn about portraits, landscapes, architecture, colour, line and shape, and Leonardo.

www.sanford-artedventures.com/play/play.html

Vermeer

Features handy clickable thumbnails of the Dutch artist's paintings along with plenty of background detail and links to more.

www.ballandclaw.com/vermeer

Techniques and workshops

Access Art

Online workshops on colour, drawing, digital photography, immersive learning space, installation art, photography, video and sculpture. Not much depth here, but plenty of inspiration.

www.accessart.org.uk

Art Techniques

Click *Creative Encyclopedia* then *Techniques* to reach pages of information about painting and pastels from famous manufacturers Winsor & Newton. It feels like a very long advert at times, but is beautifully produced.

www.winsornewton.com/index2.php

Artist's Toolkit

See animated demos of how line, colour, shape, space and balance can be used to create artwork. See videos of artists in action or have a go at art yourself with a dinky on-screen utility.

www.artsconnected.org/toolkit/index.html

Show Me

Discover how to draw, design, paint, sculpt, create and do all sorts of things with this spiffing set of hands-on activities and links.

www.show.me.uk/topicpage/Art-and-Design.html

Artyfactory

Free online workshops on African masks, Egyptian art, pencil portraits, and perspective drawing. They are well presented but not interactive.

www.artyfactory.com

Art Attack

Hey, come on – everyone loves *Art Attack!* Access shedloads of step-by-step projects using all sorts of media in 2-D and 3-D. A useful place to learn creative techniques.

www.hitentertainment.com/artattack

Techniques and Workshops

Using Perspective

An interactive site with slides, activities and key learning points. An excellent way of learning about perspective. Click *Teaching Resources*, then *KS3* then *Using Perspective*.

www.ngfl-cymru.org.uk/index-new.htm

Drawing Cartoons

Six tremendous PDFs you can download with all sorts of info and tips about drawing cartoons. There are stacks of cartoon jokes, examples of different styles, and exercises for you to try. Nice.

www.abwac.org.au/ACAkidspage.htm

Kidzone

Have a go at virtual printing, learn what makes Canaletto so admired, learn to collage and weave, or discover how living artists sculpt and use ceramics. Excellento.

www.artisancam.com/kidzone/

Galleries

The National Gallery

One of the best gallery sites: find images of great paintings organised in different ways, learn about artists, and try out some activities in the *Art Action Zone*.

www.nationalgallery.org.uk

National Portrait Gallery

Search thousands of memorable images of British people by portrait, artist or sitter.

www.npg.org.uk/live/index.asp

Tate

The Tate galleries feature British art from 1500 onwards and international modern art. Collections of paintings, drawings, photos, sculptures, ceramics and much more can be searched in different ways.

www.tate.org.uk

Galleries

Washington DC National Gallery of Art

Top-notch kids' site of this American gallery, with superior art activities, plus a guide to searching the museum's huge collection of pictures and objects from all over the world.

www.nga.gov/kids/kids.htm

The Louvre

This museum contains over 35,000 exhibits and you can see examples of Egyptian, Roman and Islamic art among the great paintings and sculptures. Click *English* first!

www.louvre.fr/llv/commun/home_flash.jsp

24-Hour Museum

Describes itself as a gateway to 3000-plus museums, galleries and heritage sites. The navigation's not the easiest, but you can search for galleries or art exhibitions around the country.

www.24hourmuseum.org.uk

The Guggenheim Collection

Search this stunning collection of mainly twentieth century abstract art from one of the US's most prominent galleries, by artist, title, date, movement, medium or concept.

www.guggenheimcollection.org/index.html

Web Museum Paris

The basic navigation here makes it an easy job to find information about artists and movements from Gothic painting to Pop Art. It includes some large images of pictures and a lot of text.

www.ibiblio.org/wm/paint/

Web Gallery of Art

Here is a searchable database of European painting and sculpture (up to mid nineteenth century). The pictures are excellent high-resolution images which can be sent as postcards, and there are artist biographies.

www.wga.hu/index.html

miscellaneous

KS3 Artwork

The homepage here is a bit baffling but the site features good-quality artwork by students of different ages, including Year 7-to-9, displayed to inspire. There are some excellent pictures along with student comments.

www.juliastubbs.co.uk

Drawing Power

Website of the Campaign for Drawing. Includes a great set of quotes entitled *Why Draw?* and info on Big Draw! events across the UK which promote drawing.

www.drawingpower.org.uk

Zoomable Pictures

Learn about painting techniques by getting a close up view of some of the National Gallery's most famous works.

www.nationalgallery.org.uk/education/visits/resources.htm

For clipart, see page 84 in the ICT section

RE

General Sites

RE Online

RE Online provides pages of links for you to
find out about Christianity, Judaism, Islam, Hinduism,
Sikhism and Buddhism. Click *Themes and Topics* first.

http://ks3.reonline.org.uk/

People of Faith

Fact files about seven major religions, plus videos
of believers talking about their faith. There are
well-illustrated articles too, giving different
perspectives.

http://pof.reonline.org.uk/

Religious Festivals

A no-frills guide to the main festivals of the major
religions. It includes facts, photographs and lots of
very handy weblinks, if you need more.

www.bbc.co.uk/schools/religion/

Christianity

Christianity

Click on *Christianity* for a clear basic introduction to the faith: no pictures but lots of helpful text.

www.world-faiths.com

Educhurch

Excellent visual website which features three different UK churches. Includes tours of the buildings, pics, videos, information plus some good interactive features.

www.educhurch.org.uk

RE:Quest

Wow! There is an incredible amount of good stuff here about Christianity. Find songs, video clips and amazing virtual tours of churches as well as all the facts you need.

www.request.org.uk

Christianity

Thinkquest: Christianity

Easy-to-use site which has sections on Jesus, Paul, baptism, the Eucharist, resurrection, and the Bible, amongst others.

http://library.thinkquest.org/28505/christianity/intro.htm

Christianity Comes to Britain

You might get lost here due to the crummy navigation, but there is a good summary of the theme and some useful photos and illustrations.

www.world-faiths.com/Year%208%20Projects/
christianity_comes_to_britain.htm

Christmas Pages

The graphics are grim, and the music drives you nuts, but there is a lot of information here about Christmas traditions and Christmas customs around the world. Turn the sound off!

http://atschool.eduweb.co.uk/carolrb/christmas/christmas1.html

Online Bible

Search the whole Bible using this efficient American site. There are different versions of the text to choose from and you can also click links to find particular chapters.

www.biblegateway.com/passage/?search=

Easter

This is a bit of a hotch-potch but there are sections on art, Lent, scripture, sermons, Jerusalem and Easter around the world.

www.makedisciples.com/Easter/

Creation

A striking animation attempting to illustrate the first few verses of the Book of Genesis from the Bible, describing God's creation.

www.k4t.com/eng_creation.htm

Judaism

Judaism for Children

Sound introduction to the Jewish faith. The site design is a bit iffy but there's plenty of helpful information and some photographs, along with links to other sites.

http://atschool.eduweb.co.uk/carolrb/judaism/judai1.html

Judaism

Comprehensive summary of the faith from the BBC. Sections on customs, beliefs, holy days, worship and history amongst others. Recommended.

www.bbc.co.uk/religion/religions/judaism/index.shtml

The Jewish Connection

A well-constructed site which centres on four Jewish people from Stoke on Trent. There are answers to basic questions about their faith and links to more information.

www.spirit-staffs.co.uk/synagogue/index1.htm

Hanukkah

A breezy introduction to the Jewish festival of lights, Hanukkah. Plenty of info, along with pictures and songs to listen to. There's a good glossary too.

www.ort.org/ort/edu/festivals/hanukkah/index.html

Sacred Writings

Find out about the Torah and other important books of the Jewish religion. Good facts but not a graphic in sight, sadly.

www.world-faiths.com/Judaism/sacred_writings.htm

Virtual Tours of Synagogues

Here are four tours to choose from, each with stacks of pictures and facts about the main Jewish place of worhip.

http://ks3.reonline.org.uk/teens_vtours.php?j

Hinduism

Hinduism for Schools

The content is confusing in places, but there is a good index here and enough illustrations to make it worthwhile.

www.btinternet.com/~vivekananda/schools1.htm

Introduction to Hinduism

BBC guide to Hinduism, which features audio files of radio programmes where believers and experts talk about the faith.

www.bbc.co.uk/worldservice/people/features/world_religions/hinduism.shtml

Hindu Beliefs

Broadband is essential to use this cartoony site – someone's gone a bit overboard with Flash. There is a glossary and lots of learning resources to try out, however.

www.hindukids.org/learn

Hindu Temple Tour

High-quality and high-tech, this site offers a
video tour of a Hindu temple, interactive pictures,
information and stories. Click *Subjects* then *RE KS2*
then *Gujurat Hindu Temple*.

www.cleo.net.uk

Hindu Worship

Clear explanation of Hindu worship and many
other aspects of the faith. No pictures, but there
is a separate page of clipart and another page
of links.

www.world-faiths.com/Hinduism/HINDUISM.HTM

Hindu Festivals

Nice and simple set of pages devoted to the
main Hindu festivals such as Holi and Diwali
(called Deepavali here).

http://library.thinkquest.org/11719/vasishtfiles/hinduopen.html

islam

Islam 4 Schools

Find out about Allah, being a Muslim, prayer, prophets, holidays, children in Islam, and tons more, with a simple question-and-answer approach.

www.islam4schools.com/high.htm

BBC Newsround Special: Islam

Top-rate guide to Islam featuring lots of clear explanations of the faith plus pictures, videos, news reports and more.

http://news.bbc.co.uk/cbbcnews/hi/specials/2005/islam/

Introduction to Islam

Plain presentation of information about origins, beliefs, traditions, worship, God, the Qur'an, the Five Pillars and more.

www.world-faiths.com

Mosques

A page of links to sites which will take you on virtual tours of mosques and other important Muslim buildings.

http://ks3.reonline.org.uk/teens_vtours.php?i

Islam Glossary

If you want to know your 'hijabs' from your 'hadiths' then click *Islam* from the *Religions* list and click *Glossary*.

www.bbc.co.uk/religion/

The Hajj

Impressive site about the big annual Muslim pilgrimage to Mecca. You can try the animated 'virtual Hajj', read about its history, see videos and more.

www.channel4.com/life/microsites/H/hajj/

Sikhism

Sikhism

Good basic introduction to the faith, with plenty of facts but not many pictures. Click the links to find out more about Gurus.

www.bbc.co.uk/schools/religion/sikhism/

Introduction to Sikhism

Uncluttered facts about the traditions, beliefs and festivals of the faith. To find pictures, click the links on the left – but beware, the *Sikh Website* links are not very helpful.

www.world-faiths.com/Sikhism/sikhism.htm

Sikhism for Children

The illustrations here are shocking, but the navigation is good and everything is presented in easily digestible short chunks.

http://atschool.eduweb.co.uk/carolrb/sikhism/sikhism1.html

Watford Sikh Gurdwara

Virtual tour of a Sikh place of worship. Strong on photos, if weak on facts.

www.thegrid.org.uk/learning/re/pupil/sikh/

The Story of Rajni

Interactive Flash presentation telling about the Sikh Golden Temple. Click *Subjects* then *RE KS3* then *The Story of Rajni*.

www.cleo.net.uk

Sikh Festivals

A dull but info-rich page about the various Sikh festivals and ceremonies held at different times. The rest of this website is worth exploring to find out about other aspects of Sikhism.

www.sikhs.org/fest.htm

Buddhism

Buddhism

Very helpful introduction to the Buddhist faith with sections on the Buddha, main teachings, the Three Yanas, temples and more. There is a glossary too.

http://education.cant.ac.uk/renet/Buddhism/FRONT.HTM

The Basics of Buddhism

BBC site which includes large audio files of radio programmes, featuring followers of Buddhism talking about the faith. Lots of information too, but not always easy to read or understand.

www.bbc.co.uk/worldservice/people/features/world_religions/buddhism.shtml

Dharma for Kids

Well-presented stories, explanations and activities which tell you about Buddha, plus the practices and beliefs of the Buddhist community.

www.dharmaforkids.com/

Being a Buddhist

Find out what it's like to be a Buddhist by reading this set of statements from a young follower of the faith and an older believer.

http://pof.reonline.org.uk/buddhism.php

What is Buddhism?

The Q&A format here is a bit tiresome but it covers interesting topics such as vegetarianism, rebirth, fate and wisdom. Worth a peek.

www.buddhanet.net/qanda.htm

Tour a Buddhist Monastery

A good collection of photos here with an interactive map, but the lack of accompanying information is a shame.

www.thegrid.org.uk/learning/re/pupil/buddhisttrail/1.shtml

MUSiC

General Sites

Music at School

This UK site offers online lessons, games, quizzes and links, although not too much actual information. There is a homework help section too.

www.musicatschool.co.uk

The Music Room

Excellent interactive information about orchestras, instruments, composers and much more. There are audio files to hear music plus games to play, and it's well designed.

www.dsokids.com/2001/rooms/musicroom.asp

BBC Children's Music

Check out what the BBC provides in terms of resources for music including facts, pictures, audio files, activities, and games where you can compose your own pieces.

www.bbc.co.uk/music/childrens/

General Sites

MUSIC

Music Notes

A comprehensive site with material on music theory, music history, styles, professions and instruments. The Java games are fairly boring though.

http://library.thinkquest.org/15413

Music Encyclopaedia

There are some superb illustrations of instruments here plus stacks of information about music and composers.

http://library.thinkquest.org/10400/html/

Composers

If you need information about the lives of the great composers such as Mozart, Bach or Vivaldi, this page has links to helpful sites.

www.cdli.ca/CITE/composer.htm

investigating music

NYP Kidzone

Essential site from the New York Philharmonic Orchestra. It has a composers' gallery with information, an instrument section where you can hear music, games, instrument-making workshops, and lots more. Ace.

http://www.nyphilkids.org/main.phtml

Music by Arrangement

You can download free sheet music for recorders and other instruments from this site. The pages are in PDF format so you'll need the free Adobe Acrobat Reader.

www.musicbyarrangement.co.uk/schoolband/

Musical Mysteries

You'll enjoy this gamey site from the BBC – it has some good animated activities to help you learn about rhythm and mood, amongst other things.

www.bbc.co.uk/northernireland/schools/4_11/music/mm/index.shtml

investigating music

Essentials of Music

A good place for researching musical eras and composers. There are 70 biographies in addition to info about music of the Middle Ages, Renaissance, Baroque, Classical, Romantic and twentieth century periods.

www.essentialsofmusic.com

Play Music

Dinky little site with facts about orchestra instruments and audio files to hear them. You'll like the simple, colourful design too.

www.playmusic.org/stage.html

The Street

A good way to learn about music of different cultures: there are five musical families from five different countries on this street. Click the instruments to find out about their music and hear samples of it.

www.bbc.co.uk/radio3/world/onyourstreet/thestreet/

Music Glossary

Explanations of hundreds of musical terms from 'accelerando' to 'xylophone'.

www.naxos.com/mgloss.htm

Drum Kits and Rhythms

Cool site all about drums and rhythm, featuring pictures, videos, sounds and links to games and activities.

www.hitchams.suffolk.sch.uk/ictmusic/drums/index.htm

The Music Room

Click *Capistrano* then *The Music Room* to access this useful site. It covers a very broad range of topics including women in music, melody, texture, medieval music and a lot more.

www.empire.k12.ca.us

♪ investigating music

Classical Timeline

Superb clickable timeline featuring musical eras from the fourteenth century to the 1900s. It has biographies of composers and lists of their works.

www.classicalarchives.com/timeline.html

JS Bach

Everything you need to know about this German meister composer. It has a searchable database of works plus an illustrated biography and timeline.

www.jsbach.org

Sheet Music Archive

Download free sheet music by composers including Beethoven, Elgar, Handel, Rossini, and Verdi.

www.sheetmusicarchive.net/index.cfm

Composing

Music Games

Here is a set of fun games from the BBC which allow you to make music. Try the *Beatmachine* for percussion or the cool *Composer* to create your own piece to email.

www.bbc.co.uk/music/childrens/games/index.shtml

Creating Music

Try some composing using a range of simple-to-use online activities. You might need to install some special Quicktime software for it to work (instructions are given).

www.creatingmusic.com/

Making Tracks

An interactive online studio with four activities where you can have a go at creating your own music.

www.bbc.co.uk/radio3/makingtracks/studio.shtml

M U S I C

♪ Understanding Music

Music Theory

Cor – this epic site has free online lessons which teach you all about the theory of music from the most basic areas to much more advanced levels. There are interactive tests too.

www.musictheory.net/

Introduction to Reading Music

This site takes you through the basics of music notation step by step, and has a neat feature where you can listen to the music displayed in each section.

http://datadragon.com/education/reading

Music Sense

Stylish little interactive guide to what's what in music. Hear notes, play with pitch, mess about with chords and scales.

www.bbc.co.uk/music/parents/activities/musicsense/index.shtml

PE

General Sites

BBC Sports Academy

A good place to go if you want to sharpen up your skills or find out about techniques. There are videos with tips by top players and athletes, sections on rules and equipment, and much more.

http://news.bbc.co.uk/sport1/hi/academy/default.stm

CBBC Sport

Although aimed also at younger children, there are useful links to games, interviews with sports players and a handy section of facts about over 100 different sports.

www.bbc.co.uk/cbbc/sport/index.shtml

Our Kids Sports

Basic portal site with useful links for the sports listed. Navigation is odd: the links appear on the right-hand side when you have clicked a sport on the left.

www.ourkidsports.com

Health and Fitness

Nutrition and the Athlete

Straightforward-but-wordy guide to how fitness is affected by diet. It covers in detail the effect on the body of alcohol, caffeine, carbohydrates and vitamins. Click *Physical Activity and Exercise* on the drop-down menu under *Healthy Lifestyles* then scroll down.

www.bupa.co.uk/health_information/html/healthy_living/lifestyle/exercise/diet_exercise/index.html

Kids' Health

Solid advice from the BBC about looking after your body. Includes an animated tour of the body and notes about healthy eating, exercise and drugs.

www.bbc.co.uk/health/kids/

Kidnetic

Excellent American site all about health and active living. Don't miss the amazing *Move Mixer* dance game where you have to design a dance then join in.

www.kidnetic.com/

Health and Fitness

LifeBytes

Click *Physical Activity* to reach information and advice about fitness. It has games, physical exercises to try, facts and a quiz, all wrapped up in a funky design.

www.lifebytes.gov.uk/index_flash.html

BAM!

Flashy site which covers physical activity, healthy eating, diseases, safety and body information. Try the *Motion Commotion* test to see what sports could be right for you. (Warning: it's very American!)

http://www.bam.gov/

Boots Learning Store

Well-presented information about health for ages 11-to-14. It doesn't cover fitness but includes sections on smoking, alcohol and drugs.

http://bootslearningstore.com/home.htm

Dance, Gymnastics and Swimming

The Aerobics Dictionary

Clever guide to Step Aerobics moves, which uses simple animation to show you how they work, plus short descriptions. There's not too much background info though.

http://www.turnstep.com/Moves/index.html

Dance links

If you want to know about different forms of dance from around the world, this site has links to lots of useful websites. Don't expect anything else though.

www.sapphireswan.com/dance

BBC Gymnastics

Unfortunately there are few good sites providing information about gymnastics. This one at least has videos of demonstrations and links to some useful sites including British Gymnastics.

http://news.bbc.co.uk/sport1/hi/other_sports/gymnastics/default.stm

Dance, Gymnastics and Swimming

Gymnastics Glossary

Find out what a 'kip' is and learn about handsprings.
A simple dictionary with some video links.

www.usa-gymnastics.org/gymnastics/glossary.html

Swimming

Scan the page for links to animations showing you
the strokes. Also has tips from top swimmers,
facts, and links to other useful sites. Excellent.

http://news.bbc.co.uk/sport1/hi/other_sports/swimming/default.stm

Swimming Strokes

Information about techniques for the major
swimming strokes. It's not very clearly presented
but scroll down and you should get there.

www.pponline.co.uk/encyc/0849.htm

Games

Netball Links

Need to know about netball? This page has links to sites about the game including rules, equipment, facts, leagues, organisations, coaching hints and more.

http://www.ucl.ac.uk/~uczcw11/baseres.htm

Football Skills

Become better than Ronaldinho with this top-class set of resources from the BBC. There are video masterclasses from top players, animations of skills and loads more.

www.bbc.co.uk/juniorfootball/

Footy4kids

Lots about coaching here but you'll also find articles on lots of other topics such as health and safety, and the history of the game. Click *Site Map* to improve the dire navigation.

www.footy4kids.co.uk

Games

Discover Rugby

Great little site with videos of techniques and skills, plus facts about the sport, games, and help with finding a club or coaching.

http://oldwww.scottishrugby.org/discoverrugby/

Raw Tennis

RAW is a tennis skills programme from the Lawn Tennis Association. You need to register to get full value from the website.

www.rawtennis.net

Youth Athletics

Click *Event Information* for an introduction to track and field events. The site will also help you find out about clubs and events in your area and has links to information sites.

www.boja.org/

other sports

Cricket links

Humungous set of links covering everything you'll ever need to know about the game and more.

http://sportsvl.com/ball/cricket/cricket.htm

Hockey online

Click on *Young People* for helpful pages on this official hockey site. It includes info about how to play and where to find local courses so you can learn more.

www.hockeyonline.co.uk

BBC Olympics

Facts about Olympic sports such as archery, badminton, cycling, fencing, rowing, sailing, volleyball and many more, with helpful links.

http://news.bbc.co.uk/sport1/hi/other_sports/4306126.stm

Languages

General Sites

Homework High

Click on *Languages* then browse or search for what you need help with in French, German or Spanish. A superb site.

www.channel4.com/learning/microsites/H/homeworkhigh

C4 Modern Languages

Two sets of fun interactive tasks to help you with German or French. The design is very funky but the sound will do your head in after a while.

www.ltscotland.org.uk/5to14/c4modernlanguages

Zut!

Fantastic on-screen activities to sharpen up your French, German, Spanish or Welsh. Each site is split into work for Y7, Y8 and Y9 and covers a wide range of topics. The business!

http://zut.languageskills.co.uk

French

Fusée

Interactive site to accompany the Fusée French course books, but useful even if you don't use them. Includes excellent activities.

www.fusee.co.uk/

French Revision

Useful listening, reading and writing exercises which use Real Player audio and Java. The audio may be slow to load, so be patient.

www.frenchrevision.co.uk

Online French Course

Free basic web course in the French language with nine lessons plus a vocabulary page. There are audio files for pronunciation, but no frills.

www.jump-gate.com/languages/french

French Steps

Excellent BBC resource in the form of a short beginner's course. It has video clips, audio files and effective short activities to work through as you go.

www.bbc.co.uk/languages/french/lj

Real French

Grammar and vocabulary help at three different levels, including games and activities. There are many other features here worth exploring too.

www.realfrench.net

French Dictionary

Translates English words into French, Spanish or Italian (and the other way round). Make sure you spell the word correctly when you type it!

www.wordreference.com

German

German Steps

Another great little language micro-site from the BBC. Learn phrases using video clips and interactive tasks based on common everyday situations such as taking a bus.

www.bbc.co.uk/languages/german/lj

German for Travellers

You don't have to be a traveller to benefit from the many high-quality learning features on this site. As well as online grammar and vocab you can learn about German culture and see piccies.

www.germanfortravellers.com

German Pronunciation

A simple, easy-to-navigate site with a guide to German pronunciation (with audio) and grammar (with on-screen exercises to practise).

www.wm.edu/modlang/gasmit/pronunciation

Spanish

Spanish Steps

BBC Spanish mini-course for beginners. It has a very effective learning system with video clips, key vocabulary and phrases, plus short online exercises to do as you go along.

www.bbc.co.uk/languages/spanish/lj/index.shtml

Alien Language

Brush up on your Spanish (or French or German) using the activities on this cracking little site from King Edward VI High School designed to teach about parts of the body.

www.alienlanguage.co.uk

Español Extra

Spanish language site with loads of nice interactive games plus recordings of Spanish speakers for listening exercises. Recommended.

www.espanol-extra.co.uk

PShe & Citizenship

PSHE

There4me.com

This site from the NSPCC provides confidential online advice for teenagers. A good place to go if you have a worry or problem.

www.there4me.com

Boots Learning Store

Information about topics such as puberty, drugs, smoking, reproduction, menstruation and alcohol. Good-quality, Flash-based slide presentations.

www.bootslearningstore.com

One Life

Worried about body image? Need to think about confidence? Studying relationships? Want to learn about bereavement or parenthood? Try this superb site from Radio 1.

www.bbc.co.uk/radio1/onelife/personal/index.shtml

PSHE

ASH

'ASH' stands for 'Action on Smoking and Health'. The site has lots of information and data about tobacco and the dangers of smoking. Unfortunately much of the material is hard to read.

www.ash.org.uk

FASA Online

Very flashy website about drugs. Once you have solved the mystery of how the site works you may access some of the useful information it offers. Watch out for the unreadable white text though!

www.fasaonline.org

Dare Teens

This site deals with the issue of drugs. There is a well written, illustrated A-Z of drugs, plus an addict's diary, and broader information about healthy living.

www.dareteens.co.uk

Bullying.co.uk

A comprehensive set of pages about bullying with plenty of advice for dealing with the issue, plus a wider look at ways to prevent bullying.

www.bullying.co.uk

The Anti-Bullying Network

Facts and advice about bullying, well-packaged, with lots of links to other sites covering topics such as text-bullying.

www.antibullying.net

Kids' Health

American site which provides facts and help about a wide range of health issues including healthy eating, mental health and illness. It's a bit babyish in places.

www.kidshealth.org/kid

See also the Science and PE sections for websites on health

Citizenship

Citizen X

Excellent introduction to the subject of citizenship from the BBC, beginning with the question of 'What is a citizen?' The site explores citizenship at local, national and global levels.

www.bbc.co.uk/schools/citizenx

Citizenship Foundation

Click *Young People* for resources dealing with money, politics, rights, hunting, identity cards and many more issues.

www.citizenshipfoundation.org.uk

Citizen Power

Plenty to get you thinking here: facts, opinions and activities all about topics such as power, rights, animal welfare, voting, war and crime.

www.channel4.com/learning/microsites/C/citizenpower/index2.htm

Newsround Guides

Brief but useful introductions to over 100 diverse topics including: school uniform, asylum seekers, GM foods, disability, vegetarianism, wristbands, obesity, terrorism and Elvis. (Yes, Elvis!)

http://news.bbc.co.uk/cbbcnews/hi/guides/default.stm

Britkid

Powerfully presented, challenging site addressing the issue of racism in Britain today. Gives you a rare chance to see life through the eyes of different cultures. Well worth a look.

www.britkid.org

Get Involved

Citizenship site showing how you can get involved in what's going on in your school, community and worldwide. Features eight case studies of successful projects.

www.bbc.co.uk/schools/citizenx/getinvolved/index.shtml

Citizenship

CAFOD

This Christian charity provides factsheets, other material and activities on a range of themes including debt, poverty, racism, disasters, aid, food, water, health, development, refugees and trade. Click *Schools* to find it.

www.cafod.org.uk/resources

Cool Planet

Oxfam's Cool Planet provides free materials for you to learn about global issues and shows you how you can take action to help change things for the better.

www.oxfam.org.uk/coolplanet/kidsweb/index.htm

Water Aid

Click *Learn Zone* and *11-to-14* to learn about the importance of water in the developing world. There are activities, games and case studies centres on students of your age.

www.wateraid.org

Global Gang

Killer site all about the developing world. Click *Homework Help* to find out about hunger and fair trade, or to learn about disasters and refugees. There are some cool games and quizzes too.

www.globalgang.org.uk

We Are From

Find out what it's like to live in a number of different European countries. The illustrated facts pages tell you about food, school, sport, toys and life in each land.

www.channel4.com/learning/microsites/W/wearefrom/main_flash.html

Go Get It

Careers site with worthwhile sections on key skills, knowing your own strengths and understanding what employers are looking for.

www.bbc.co.uk/northernireland/schools/11_16/gogetit/index.shtml

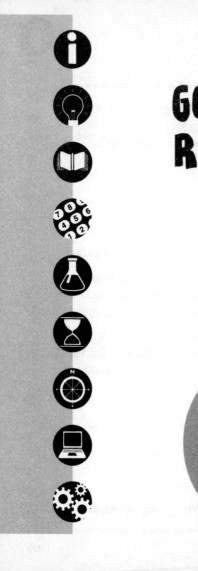

General Reference

Reference

Wikipedia

Amazingly comprehensive web encyclopedia with articles written and edited by anyone who wants to contribute. A bit short on illustrations in places, but otherwise wonderful.

http://en.wikipedia.org

Fact Monster

A good starting point if you need quick facts and information about places, people, events and so on. It includes a search engine and a homework page, but the American bias is a drag.

www.factmonster.com

Encyclopedia.com

Free encyclopedia with browsing and searching features. The results are basic but it does have a dictionary and thesaurus too.

www.encyclopedia.com

Study Skills

Homework High: Study Skills

Very good detailed notes written by teachers and organised into KS3 subjects. A must.

www.channel4.com/learning/microsites/H/homeworkhigh/study-skills.html

Onion Street

Lots of advice here on a very wide range of topics including revision, tackling tests, motivation and internet research. Well worth bookmarking.

www.bbc.co.uk/schools/communities/onionstreet/skills/

Encarta Links

Seven websites which offer help with topics such as researching on the web and making effective notes.

http://encarta.msn.com/webcenter_0.5.9/Study_Skills.html#tcsel

TOP 10 Homework Tips

TOP 10 HOMEWORK TIPS

1. Do homework sooner rather than later

Don't put it off – get it out of the way! If you leave it too long you'll only get tired and stressed and you could botch it…

2. Find a quiet place

Away from the telly and anything else which is loud and distracting, like your brother or sister.

3. Make sure you know exactly what you need to do

Read the question or task, then read it again. Go on. There's nothing worse than handing in five pages about puddings when you were supposed to write about deserts.

4. If you don't understand the task, ask!

You can often save hours of brain-ache by asking a parent or older brother or sister – especially the ones who are good at explaining things.

5. Longer projects need planning

Of course, most homework doesn't need planning, but if you do have a longer project over a holiday then sit down and decide what you need to do first and what are the priorities for your precious time. Computers can't plan for you. Discussing the project with a friend is often a fruitful idea.

6. Good presentation: it always pays off

Teachers love work which is neat, well set out, carefully illustrated and clear, even if the content is slightly dodgy. Present your work well and you're halfway there.

7. Write at a desk or table, sitting on a chair if you can

Are you one of those kids who writes essays whilst sprawled across the bed or curled up on the floor? Well don't. And don't do them in the shower either.

8. If stuck, get help

Even Einstein got stuck sometimes. If you're getting nowhere with homework, seek out someone smart at home to help you or talk to your teacher at the first opportunity – don't just pretend it's not there.

9. In your own words, please ...

You probably know that teachers go berserk if you just print something straight off a website or CD-ROM, so never be tempted. Instead, read what you find out then write your own version of it. And remember that the internet is not always right!

10. Check through what you've written

I know, adults go on and on and on and on and on about this. That's because it's right! It won't hurt you…really…go *on*.